Grade
2
Ages 7–8

Master Math at Home

Addition and Subtraction

Scan the QR code to help your child's learning at home.

DK | **MATH NO PROBLEM!**

mastermathathome.com

How to use this book

Math — No Problem! created Master Math at Home to help children develop fluency in the subject and a rich understanding of core concepts.

Key features of the Master Math at Home books include:

- Carefully designed lessons that provide structure, but also allow flexibility in how they're used.

- Speech bubbles containing content designed to spark diverse conversations, with many discussion points that don't have obvious "right" or "wrong" answers.

- Rich illustrations that will guide children to a discussion of shapes and units of measurement, allowing them to make connections to the wider world around them.

- Exercises that allow a flexible approach and can be adapted to suit any child's cognitive or functional ability.

- Clearly laid-out pages that encourage children to practice a range of higher-order skills.

- A community of friendly and relatable characters who introduce each lesson and come along as your child progresses through the series.

You can see more guidance on how to use these books at **mastermathathome.com**.

We're excited to share all the ways you can learn math!

Math — No Problem!
mastermathathome.com
www.mathnoproblem.com
hello@mathnoproblem.com

First American Edition, 2022
Published in the United States by DK Publishing
1745 Broadway, 20th Floor, New York, NY 10019

22 23 24 25 26 10 9 8 7 6 5 4 3 2 1
002–327132–Nov/2022

FSC MIX
Paper | Supporting responsible forestry
www.fsc.org FSC™ C018179

This book was made with Forest Stewardship Council™ certified paper—one small step in DK's commitment to a sustainable future. For more information go to www.dk.com/our-green-pledge

Published in Great Britain by Dorling Kindersley Limited

A catalog record for this book is available from the Library of Congress.

ISBN: 978-0-7440-5187-2
Printed and bound in China

For the curious
www.dk.com

Acknowledgments

The publisher would like to thank the authors and consultants Andy Psarianos, Judy Hornigold, Adam Gifford, Dr. Wong Khoon Yoong, Jessica Kaminski, and Dr. Anne Hermanson.

The Castledown typeface has been used with permission from the Colophon Foundry.

Contents

Ruby   Elliott   Amira   Charles   Lulu   Sam   Oak   Holly   Ravi   Emma   Jacob   Hannah

Hundreds

Starter

Charles is helping his dad put sheets of tiles on the bathroom wall. How many tiles are there in total?

Each of these sheets has 100 tiles on it.

Example

We can use these to help us count. Each of these is equal to 100.

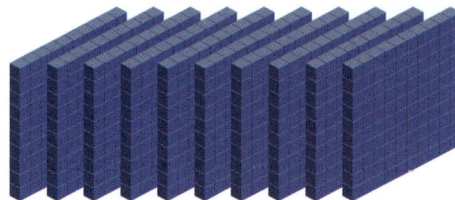

There are 10 sheets in total.

We can count in hundreds. 100, 200, 300, 400, ...

...500, 600, 700, 800, 900, 1000 We say **one thousand**.

There are 1000 tiles in total.

100   one hundred

200   two hundred

300   three hundred

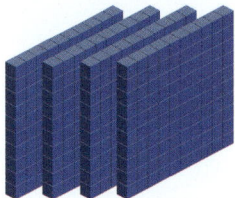

400   four hundred

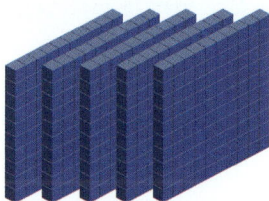

500   five hundred

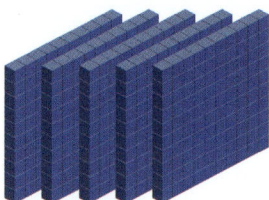

600   six hundred

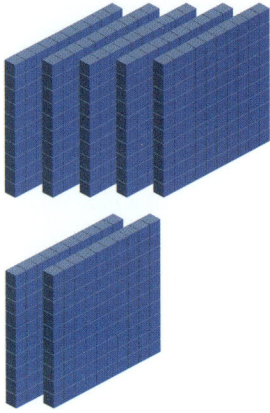

700   seven hundred

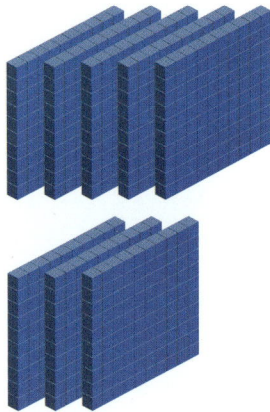

800   eight hundred

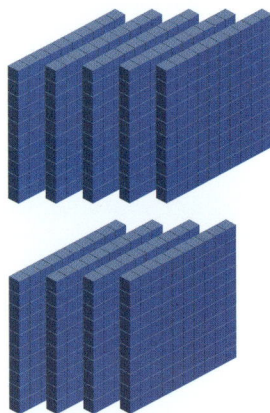

900   nine hundred

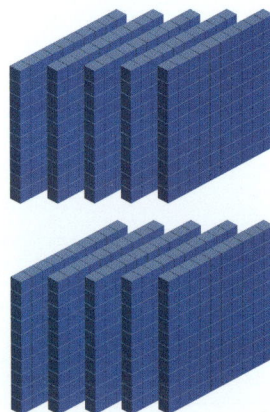

1000   one thousand

Draw lines to match.

500
five hundred

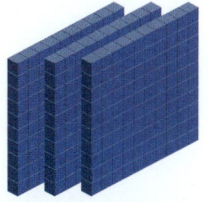

1000
one thousand

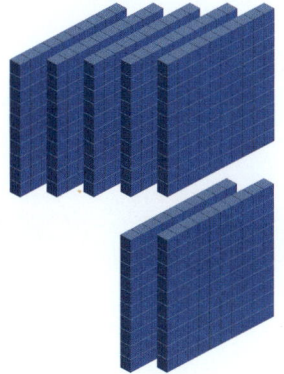

700
seven hundred

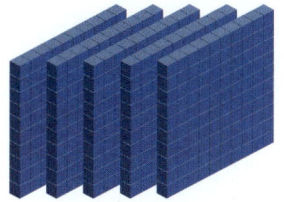

300
three hundred

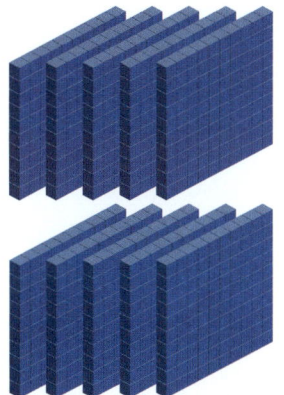

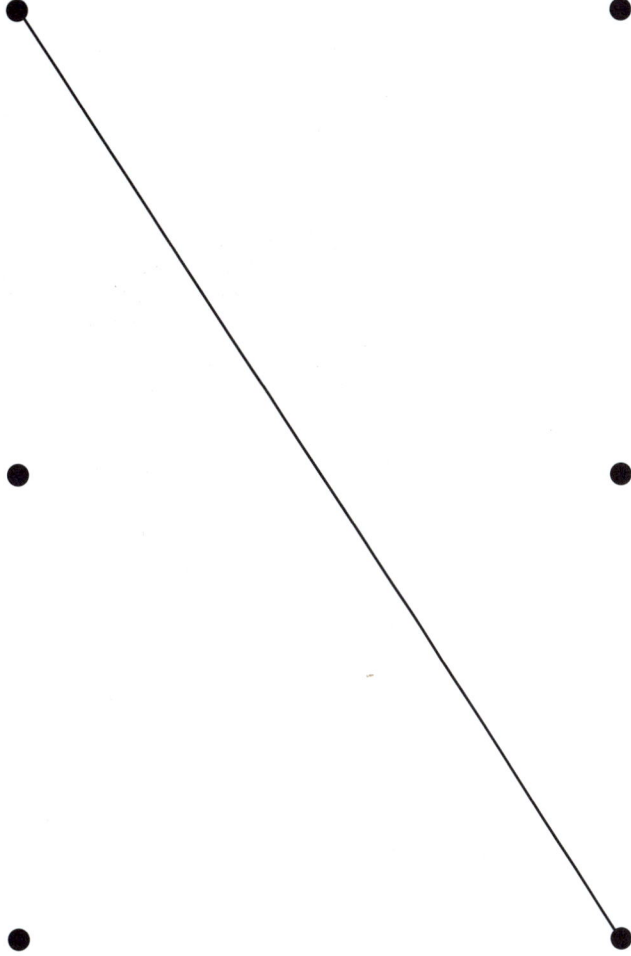

Place Value

Starter

How many cards does the shopkeeper have altogether?

Example

There are 4 boxes of cards. Each box has 100 cards in it.

There are also 3 packs of 10 cards and 5 loose cards.

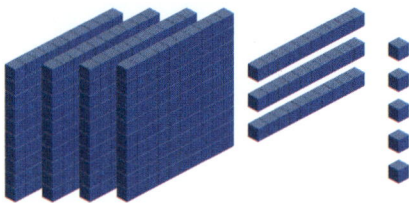

h	t	o
4	3	5

435 = 4 hundreds + 3 tens + 5 ones
435 = 400 + 30 + 5

The digit 4 stands for 4 **hundreds** or 400.
The digit 3 stands for 3 **tens** or 30.
The digit 5 stands for 5 **ones** or 5.

The shopkeeper has 435 cards.
435 is written as **four hundred and thirty-five**.

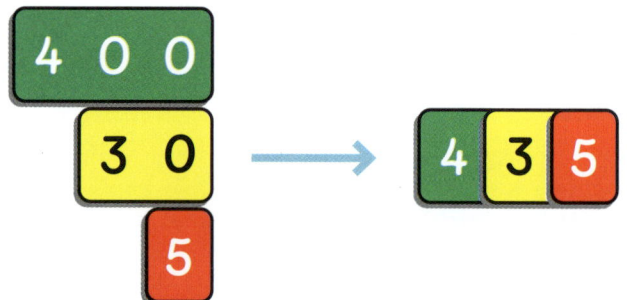

1 Count in hundreds, tens, and ones.
Fill in the blanks.

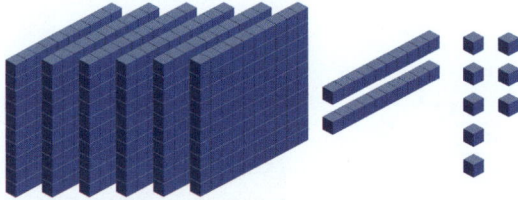

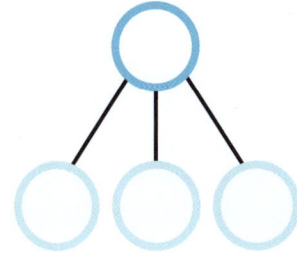

h	t	o

[ ] = [ ] hundreds + [ ] tens + [ ] ones

[ ] = [ ] + [ ] + [ ]

The value of the digit 6 is [ ] .

The digit 8 stands for [ ] .

The digit [ ] is in the tens place.

2 Write the words in numerals.

(a) seven hundred and sixty-eight [ ]

(b) two hundred and ninety-one [ ]

3 Write the numbers in words.

(a) 593 [ ]

(b) 359 [ ]

Comparing Numbers

Starter

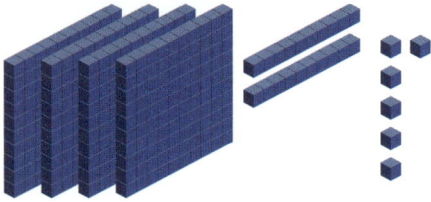

426

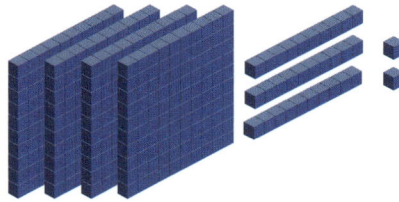

432

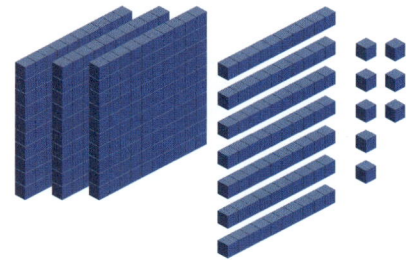

378

Which number is the greatest and which is the least?

Example

h	t	o
4	2	6

h	t	o
4	3	2

h	t	o
3	7	8

First, we should look at the hundreds. 426 and 432 both have 4 hundreds. 378 has 3 hundreds.

378 is the smallest number.

Next, we need to look at the tens. 426 has 2 tens and 432 has 3 tens. 432 has more tens. It is the greatest number.

378   426 432

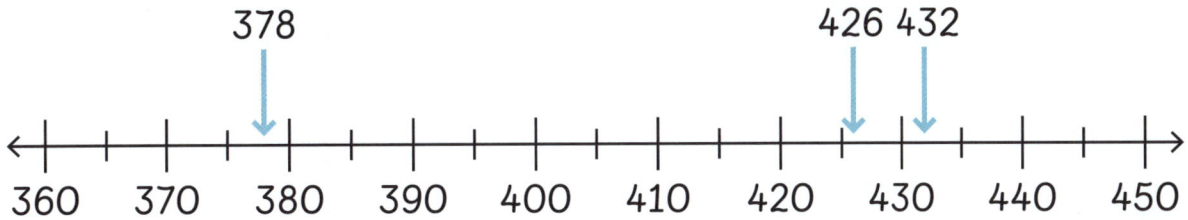

360   370   380   390   400   410   420   430   440   450

We can use a number line to check.

432 is the greatest number and 378 is the smallest number.

Practice

1 Put the numbers in order from greatest to least.

(a) 765, 675, 756

☐ , ☐ , ☐

(b) 869, 870, 868

☐ , ☐ , ☐

2 Put the numbers in order from least to greatest.

(a) 391, 412, 389

☐ , ☐ , ☐

(b) 897, 789, 879

☐ , ☐ , ☐

3 Use the digits below to make the greatest and the least 3-digit numbers.

| 3 | 2 | 7 | 9 | 6 |

☐
greatest

☐
least

Adding and Subtracting Within 20

Starter

Elliott is arranging 8 basketballs and 7 volleyballs on a cart.

How many balls are there altogether?

Example

1

First, make 10. Split 7 into 2 and 5, then add 8 and 2.

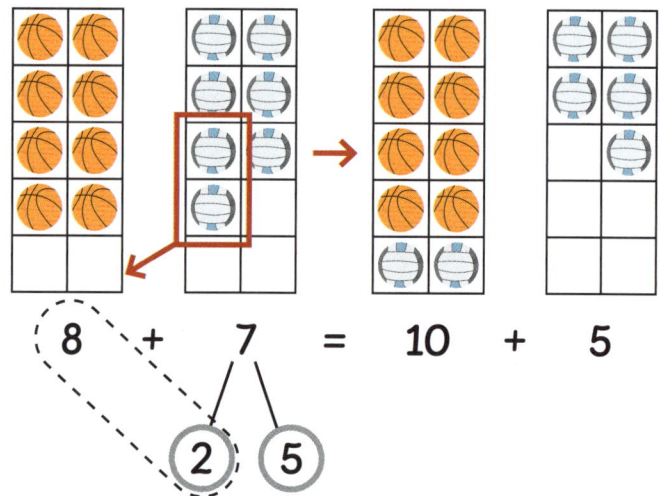

$$8 + 7 = 10 + 5$$

with 7 split into 2 and 5

There are 15 balls altogether.

2 Ruby adds 3 soccer balls to the cart. How many balls are there in all?

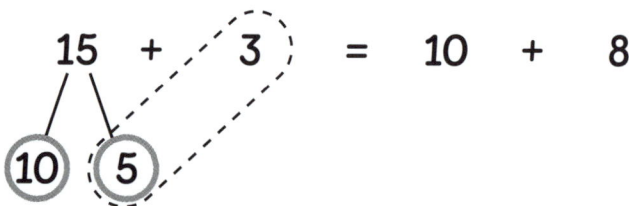

$$15 + 3 = 10 + 8$$

with 15 split into 10 and 5

First add the ones. Split 15 into 10 and 5, then add 5 and 3.

There are 18 balls in all.

3 Lulu takes out 6 balls to place in a mesh bag.
How many balls are left?

I can subtract like this.

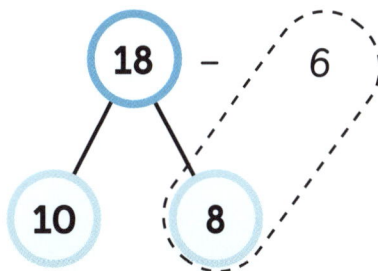

18 − 6

10   8

$8 - 6 = 2$
$10 + 2 = 12$

There are 12 balls left.

4 7 of the balls left are basketballs and the rest are volleyballs.
How many volleyballs are left?

Split 12 into 2 and 10. Then subtract 7 from the 10.

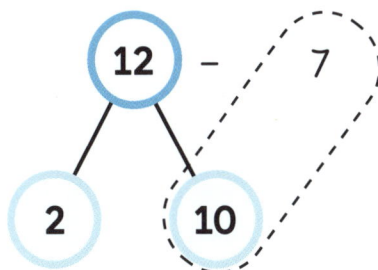

12 − 7

2   10

$10 - 7 = 3$
$2 + 3 = 5$

There are 5 volleyballs left.

Practice

1 Add.

(a) $7 + 6 =$

(b) $9 + 5 =$

(c) $13 + 3 =$

(d) $14 + 5 =$

2 Subtract.

(a) $19 - 3 =$

(b) $17 - 4 =$

(c) $15 - 8 =$

(d) $13 - 7 =$

Adding without Renaming

$63 + 4 = $ ☐

$138 + 20 = $ ☐

$565 + 300 = $ ☐

How can we add these numbers?

$63 + 4 = $

$138 + 20 = $

$565 + 300 = $

Example

For 63 + 4 we only need to add the ones.

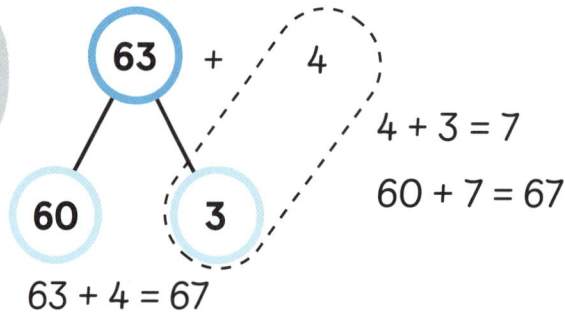

63 + 4

63 → 60, 3

$4 + 3 = 7$
$60 + 7 = 67$

$63 + 4 = 67$

	t	o
	6	3
+		4
	6	7

I can use a similar method for 138 + 20. We only need to add the tens.

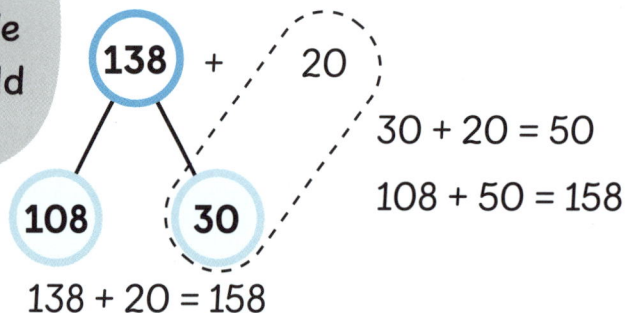

138 + 20

138 → 108, 30

$30 + 20 = 50$
$108 + 50 = 158$

$138 + 20 = 158$

	h	t	o
	1	3	8
+		2	0
	1	5	8

For 565 + 300 we only need to add the hundreds.

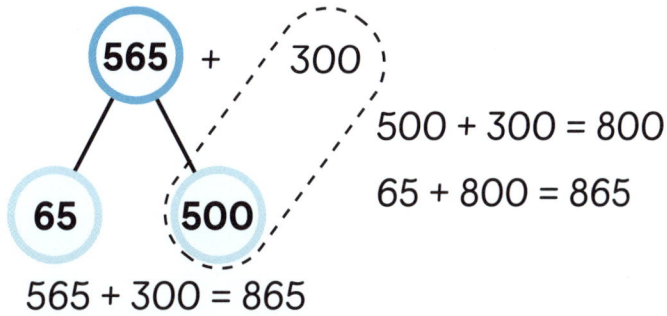

565 + 300

65   500

565 + 300 = 865

500 + 300 = 800
65 + 800 = 865

h	t	o
5	6	5
+ 3	0	0
8	6	5

Practice

1 Complete the number bonds and add.

(a) 752 + 6

750   ◯

752 + 6 = ☐

(b) 843 + 40

803   ◯

843 + 40 = ☐

(c) 634 + 200

◯   ◯

634 + 200 = ☐

2 Add and fill in the blanks.

(a) 34 + 5 = ☐

(b) 57 + 40 = ☐

(c) 221 + 30 = ☐

(d) 453 + 500 = ☐

Adding with Renaming (Part 1)

Starter

Elliott read 237 pages of his novel last week and 218 pages this week. How many pages has Elliott read in total?

Example

We need to add 237 and 218.

Step 1   Add the ones.
Rename the ones.

7 ones + 8 ones = 15 ones
15 ones = 1 ten and 5 ones

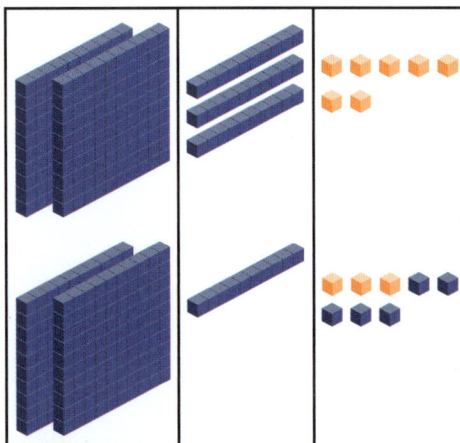

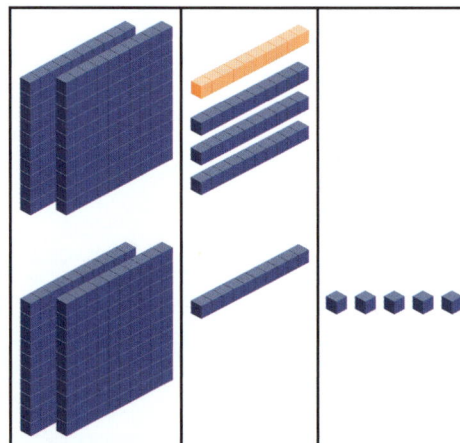

	h	t	o
	2	$\overset{1}{3}$	7
+	2	1	8
			5

Step 2   Add the tens.   1 ten + 3 tens + 1 ten = 5 tens

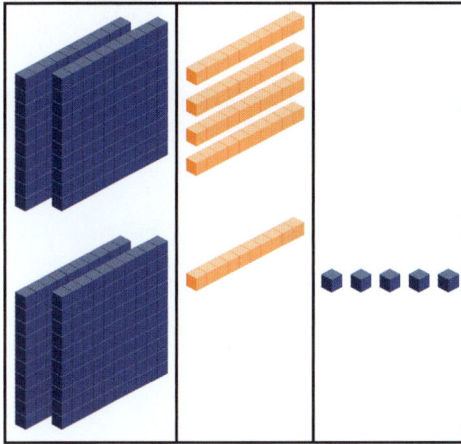

```
    h   t   o
            1
    2   3   7
+   2   1   8
_____
        5   5
_____
```

Step 3   Add the hundreds.   2 hundreds + 2 hundreds = 4 hundreds

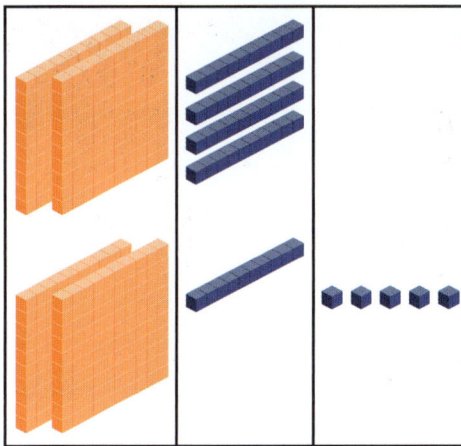

```
    h   t   o
            1
    2   3   7
+   2   1   8
_____
    4   5   5
_____
```

237 + 218 = 455

Elliott has read 455 pages in total.

Practice

Add.

1   426 and 349

h	t	o
4	2	6
+ 3	4	9

2   208 and 463

h	t	o
2	0	8
+ 4	6	3

3   569 and 319

h	t	o
5	6	9
+ 3	1	9

Adding with Renaming (Part 2)

Starter

There are 382 people waiting in line for the amusement park to open.
A bus drops off another 35 people who also join the line.

How many people are now in line for the amusement park?

Example

We need to add 382 and 35.

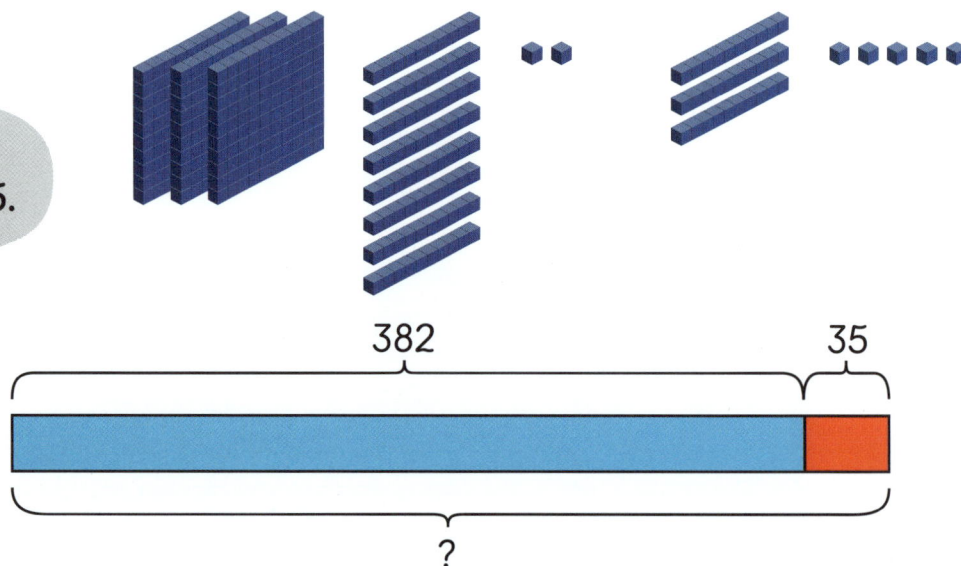

382

35

?

Add 382 and 35.

Step 1   Add the ones.

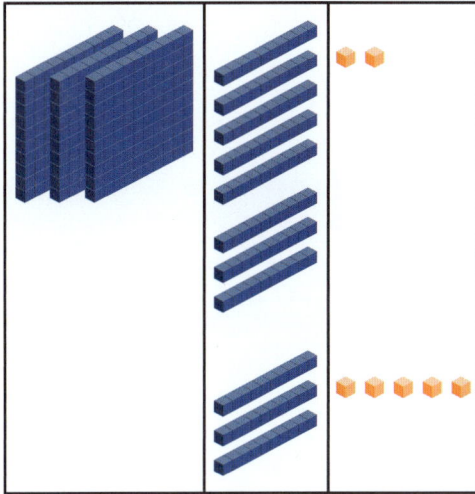

	h	t	o
	3	8	2
+		3	5
			7

Step 2   Add the tens.
8 tens + 3 tens = 11 tens
Rename the tens.
11 tens = 1 hundred + 1 ten

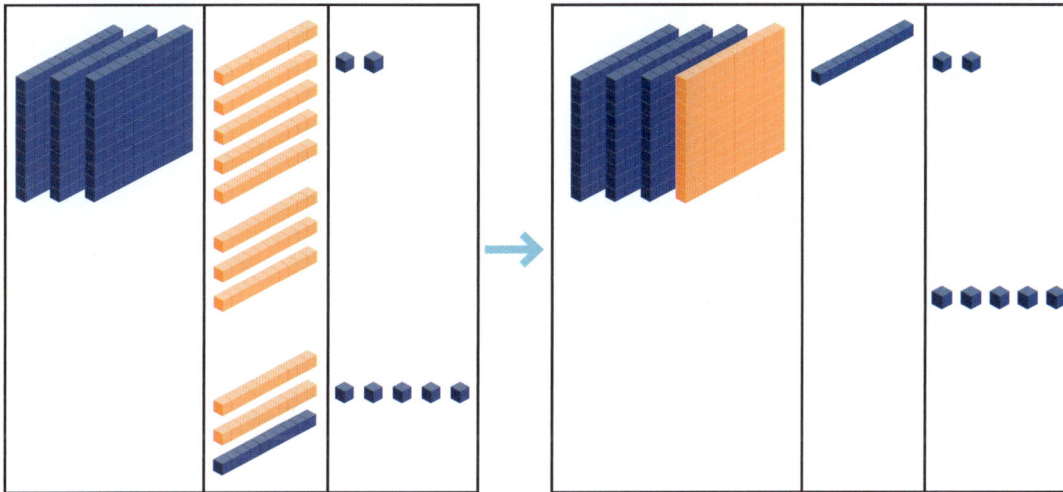

	h	t	o
	¹3	8	2
+		3	5
		1	7

Step 3   Add the hundreds.
1 hundred + 3 hundreds = 4 hundreds

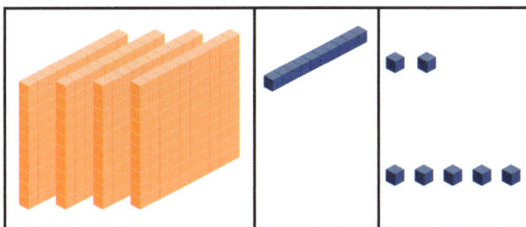

	h	t	o
	¹3	8	2
+		3	5
	4	1	7

382 + 35 = 417

There are now 417 people in line for the amusement park.

1 Add.

(a)
h	t	o
	8	0
+ 7	2	0

(b)
h	t	o
2	6	5
+	7	3

(c)
h	t	o
4	9	6
+	2	2

(d)
h	t	o
5	5	2
+	8	6

2 Add.

(a) 470 + 50 =

(b) 150 + 56 =

(c) 281 + 41 =

(d) 74 + 635 =

(e) 67 + 272 =

(f) 325 + 92 =

(g) 552 + 94 =

(h) 795 + 93 =

3 There are 251 children already sitting down for the school assembly.
58 5th Grade children then arrive and take their seats.
How many children are now sitting down?

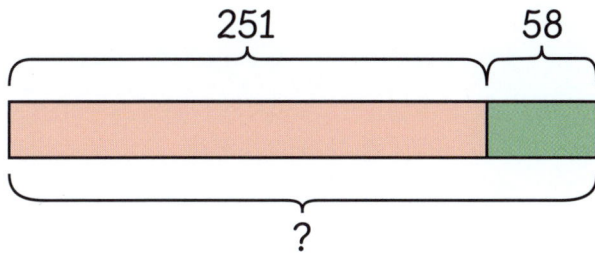

children are now sitting down.

4 Elliott has 134 more beads than Oak.
Oak has 80 beads.
How many beads does Elliott have?

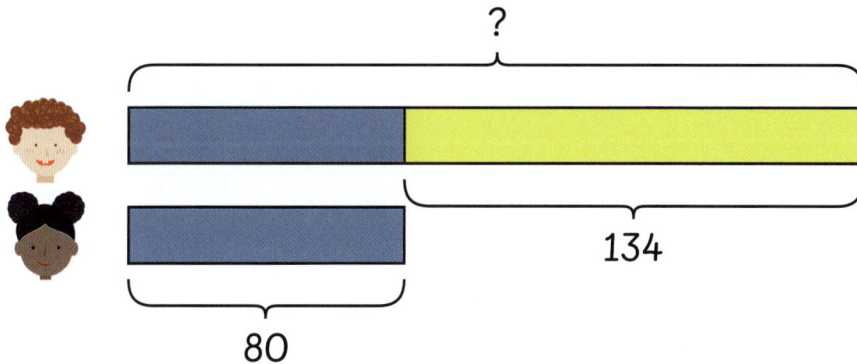

Elliott has [ ] beads.

Adding with Renaming (Part 3)

Starter

417 people bought tickets for the amusement park in the first hour. During the next hour, 294 people bought tickets.

How many tickets did the amusement park sell in the first 2 hours?

Example

417   294

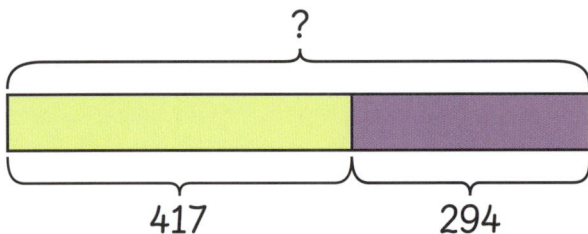

We need to add the two numbers to find the total.

Add 417 and 294.

Step 1   Add the ones.   7 ones + 4 ones = 11 ones
              Rename the ones.   11 ones = 1 ten + 1 one

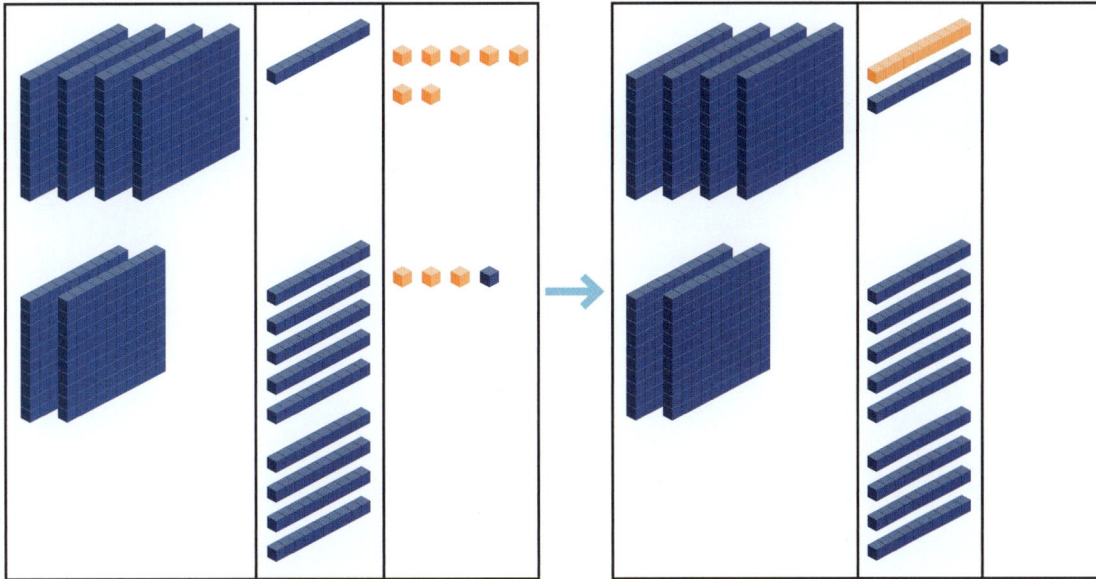

	h	t	o
	4	^{1}1	7
+	2	9	4
			1

Step 2   Add the tens.   1 ten + 10 tens = 11 tens
              Rename the tens.   11 tens = 1 hundred + 1 ten

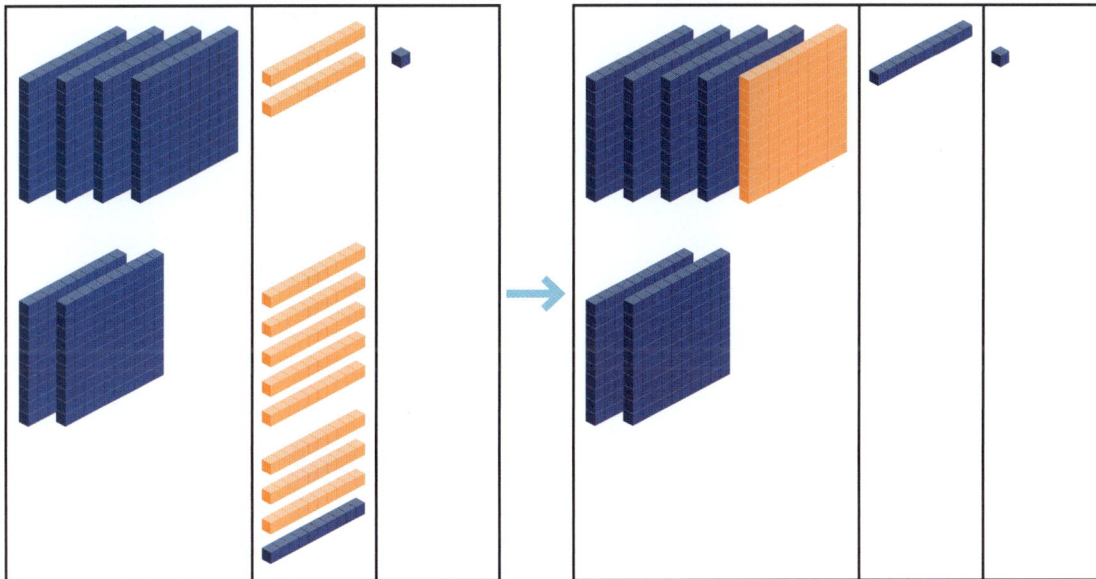

	h	t	o
	^{1}4	^{1}1	7
+	2	9	4
		1	1

23

Step 3 Add the hundreds.

1 hundred + 4 hundreds + 2 hundreds = 7 hundreds

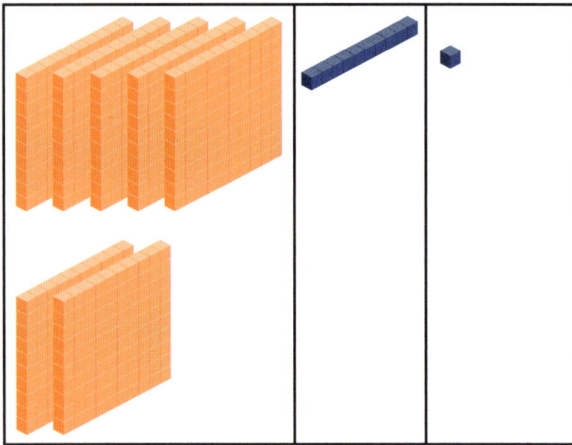

	h	t	o
	¹4	¹1	7
+	2	9	4
	7	1	1

417 + 294 = 711

The amusement park sold 711 tickets in the first 2 hours.

Practice

1 Add.

(a)

	h	t	o
	2	6	5
+	3	7	8

(b)

	h	t	o
	4	7	2
+	2	9	9

(c)

	h	t	o
	2	7	8
+	2	2	2

(d)

	h	t	o
	3	3	6
+	5	6	8

(e)

h	t	o
6	9	7
+ 1	8	7

(f)

h	t	o
2	8	9
+ 4	5	8

2 A farmer has 376 pumpkins growing on one patch of land.
She has 227 pumpkins growing on another patch.
How many pumpkins does the farmer have altogether?

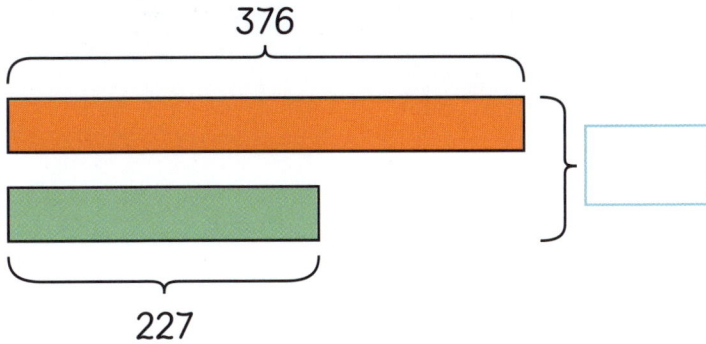

376

227

The farmer has [ ] pumpkins altogether.

3 Player A scored 177 points and Player B scored 187 points in an online soccer game. How many points did they score altogether?

The two players scored [ ] points altogether.

Adding Three or Four 2-Digit Numbers

Starter

Emma scored 45 points, 83 points, and 64 points in a video game.

What was her total score?

ROUND 1: 45 POINTS
ROUND 2: 83 POINTS
ROUND 3: 64 POINTS

Example

First, add two numbers.

	h	t	o
		4	5
+		8	3
	1	2	8

	h	t	o
	1	2¹	8
+		6	4
	1	9	2

Then, add the third number.

Emma scored 192 points in total.

We can also add the numbers in a different order.

h	t	o
	6	4
+	4	5
1	0	9

h	t	o
1	0¹	9
+	8	3
1	9	2

We get the same answer.

Practice

1 Add 43, 20, and 29.

t	o
4	3
+ 2	0

t	o
+ 2	9

43 + 20 + 29 = ☐

2 Add.

(a) 36 + 52 + 13 = ☐

(b) 76 + 72 + 35 = ☐

(c) 16 + 37 + 24 + 51 = ☐

(d) 82 + 47 + 25 + 69 = ☐

Subtracting without Renaming

76 − 4 = ☐

167 − 50 = ☐

978 − 200 = ☐

How can we subtract these numbers?

76 − 4 =

167 − 50 =

978 − 200 =

Example

For 76 − 4 you only need to subtract the ones.

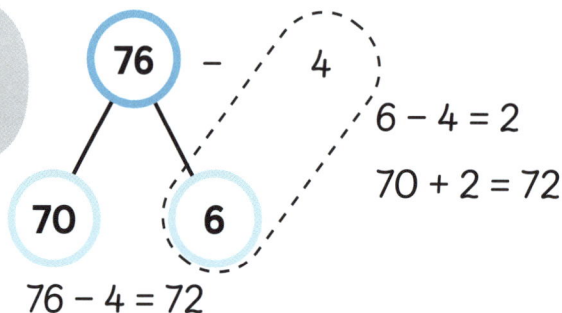

76 − 4

70   6

$6 - 4 = 2$

$70 + 2 = 72$

76 − 4 = 72

	t	o
	7	6
−		4
	7	2

For 167 − 50 we only need to subtract the tens.

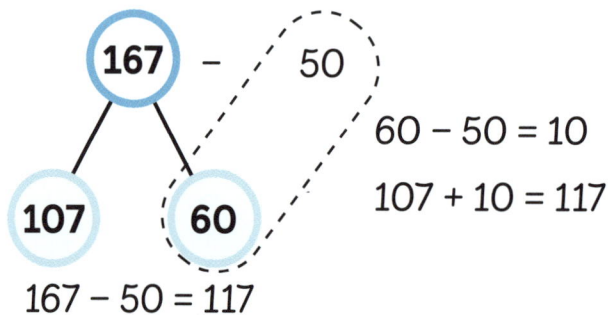

167 − 50

107   60

$60 - 50 = 10$

$107 + 10 = 117$

167 − 50 = 117

	h	t	o
	1	6	7
−		5	0
	1	1	7

For 978 − 200 we only need to subtract the hundreds.

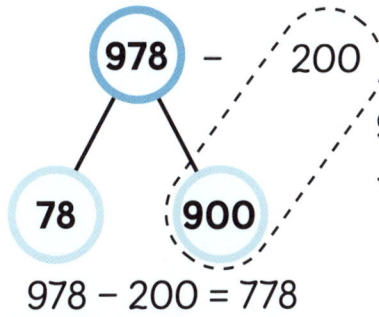

978 − 200 = 778

$$900 − 200 = 700$$
$$700 + 78 = 778$$

h	t	o
9	7	8
− 2	0	0
7	7	8

Practice

1 Complete the number bonds and subtract.

(a)

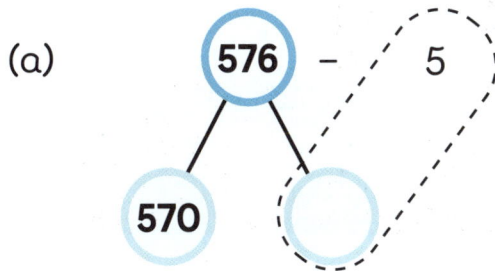

576 − 5 = ☐

(b)

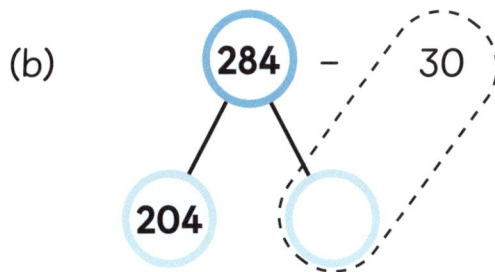

284 − 30 = ☐

(c)

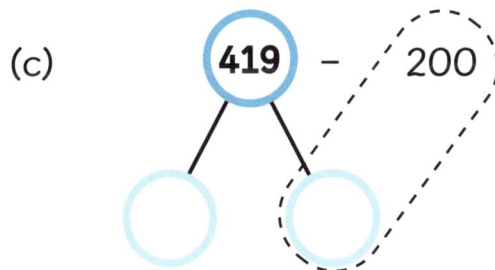

419 − 200 = ☐

2 Subtract and fill in the blanks.

(a) 57 − 6 = ☐

(b) 73 − 30 = ☐

(c) 483 − 50 = ☐

(d) 949 − 700 = ☐

Subtracting with Renaming (Part 1)

Starter

What does Oak need to do to find the answer?

Example

572

? | 56

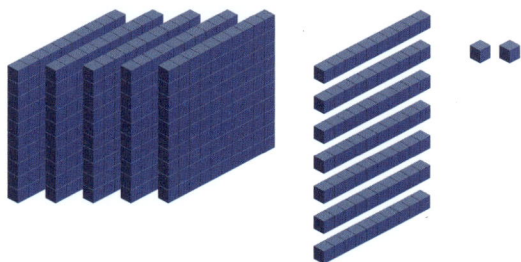

> Oak needs to subtract to find the answer but there are not enough ones in 572.

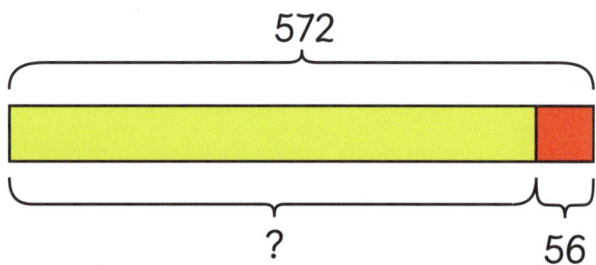

> We can rename 1 ten to 10 ones. We will then have 12 ones in total to subtract from.

Subtract 56 from 572.

Step 1   Rename 1 ten into 10 ones.
          Subtract the ones.
          12 ones – 6 ones = 6 ones

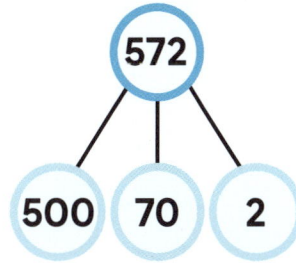

572
500   70   2

$$\begin{array}{ccc} h & t & o \\ 5 & {}^6\not{7} & {}^{12}\not{2} \\ - & 5 & 6 \\ \hline & & 6 \\ \hline \end{array}$$

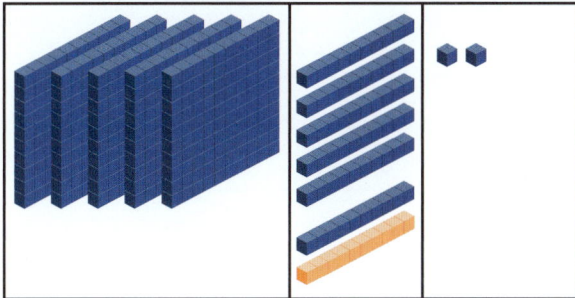

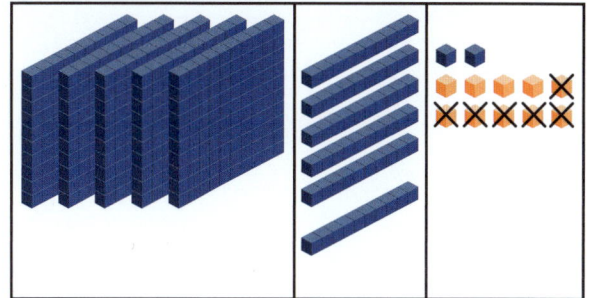

Step 2   Subtract the tens.
          6 tens – 5 tens = 1 ten

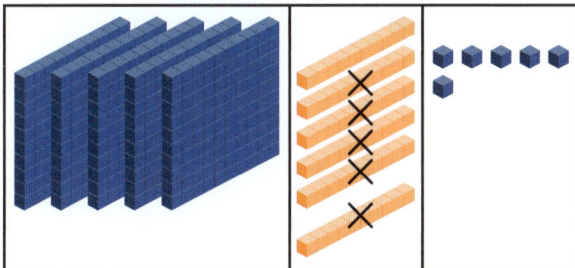

$$\begin{array}{ccc} h & t & o \\ 5 & {}^6\not{7} & {}^{12}\not{2} \\ - & 5 & 6 \\ \hline & 1 & 6 \\ \hline \end{array}$$

Step 3   Subtract the hundreds.
          5 hundreds – 0 hundreds = 5 hundreds

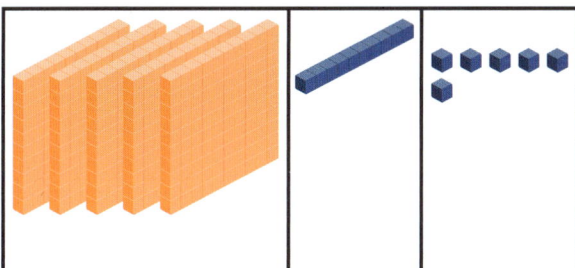

$$\begin{array}{ccc} h & t & o \\ 5 & {}^6\not{7} & {}^{12}\not{2} \\ - & 5 & 6 \\ \hline 5 & 1 & 6 \\ \hline \end{array}$$

572 – 56 = 516

1 Subtract.

(a)

h	t	o
2	7	6
−	5	9

(b)

h	t	o
7	9	3
−	2	7

(c)

h	t	o
5	3	6
− 1	2	8

(d)

h	t	o
9	5	4
− 4	3	6

(e)

h	t	o
8	7	6
− 3	0	9

(f)

h	t	o
6	9	5
− 3	5	6

2 Holly's high score in a video game is 128 points more than Ravi's high score. Holly's high score is 980 points.

(a) What is Ravi's high score in the video game?

Ravi's high score in the video game is ⬚.

(b) Charles's high score is 665 points.
What is the difference between Charles's high score
and Holly's high score?

The difference between Charles's high score and

Holly's high score is [   ].

(c) Who has more points, Ravi or Charles?

[   ] has more points.

(d) How many more points does he have?

He has [   ] more points.

Subtracting with Renaming (Part 2)

Starter

There are 506 students at Evergreen Elementary School.
142 of the children wear glasses.

How many of the children do not wear glasses?

Example

506

?   142

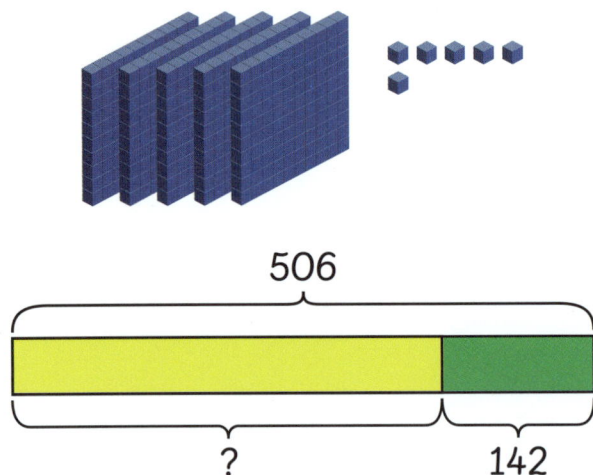

We need to subtract 142 from 506 but there are not enough tens.

We can rename 1 hundred into 10 tens.

34

Subtract 142 from 506.

Step 1   Subtract the ones.
          6 ones − 2 ones = 4 ones

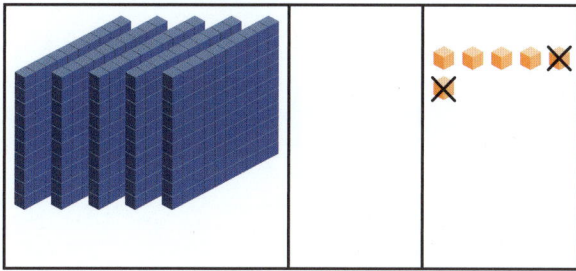

$$
\begin{array}{c c c}
h & t & o \\
5 & 0 & 6 \\
-\quad 1 & 4 & 2 \\
\hline
 & & 4 \\
\hline
\end{array}
$$

506
400 100 6

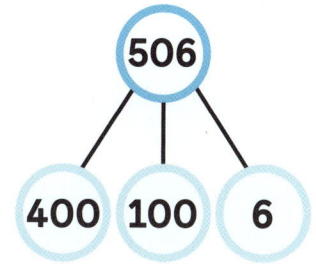

Step 2   Rename 1 hundred into 10 tens.
          Subtract the tens.
          10 tens − 4 tens = 6 tens

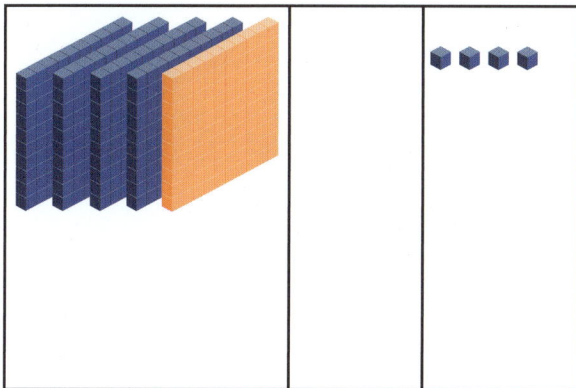

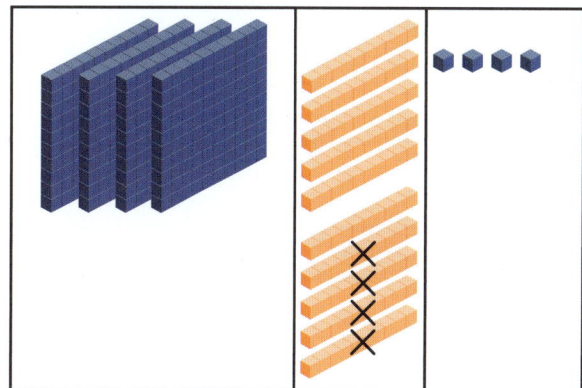

$$
\begin{array}{c c c}
h & t & o \\
\overset{4}{5} & \overset{10}{0} & 6 \\
-\quad 1 & 4 & 2 \\
\hline
 & 6 & 4 \\
\hline
\end{array}
$$

Step 3   Subtract the hundreds.
          4 hundreds − 1 hundred = 3 hundreds

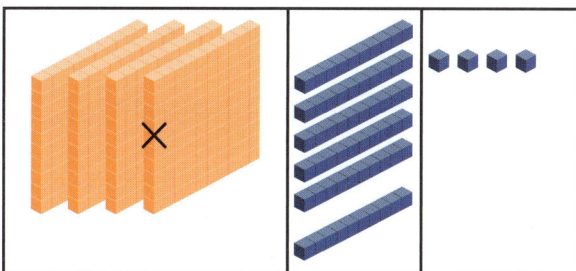

$$
\begin{array}{c c c}
h & t & o \\
\overset{4}{5} & \overset{10}{0} & 6 \\
-\quad 1 & 4 & 2 \\
\hline
3 & 6 & 4 \\
\hline
\end{array}
$$

506 − 142 = 364

364 children do not wear glasses.

Practice

1 Subtract.

(a)

h	t	o
2	5	8
−	6	3

(b)

h	t	o
7	1	9
−	4	5

(c)

h	t	o
8	4	5
− 7	5	3

(d)

h	t	o
9	1	5
− 1	6	2

(e)

h	t	o
4	4	4
− 1	7	3

(f)

h	t	o
5	6	8
− 2	8	4

2 A parking lot has 425 parking spots.
191 of the parking spots have cars
in them.
How many parking spots are empty?

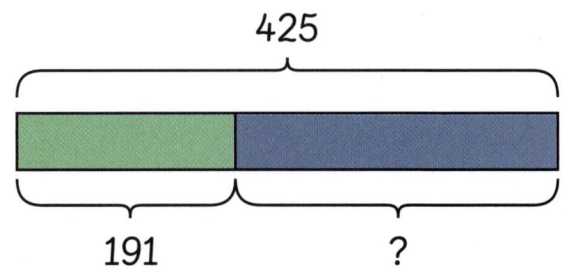

425

191   ?

There are ☐ empty parking spots in the parking lot.

36

3 (a) A snack bar sold 318 burgers in one week.
The week after, it sold 151 burgers.
How many more burgers did it sell in the first week than in the second week?

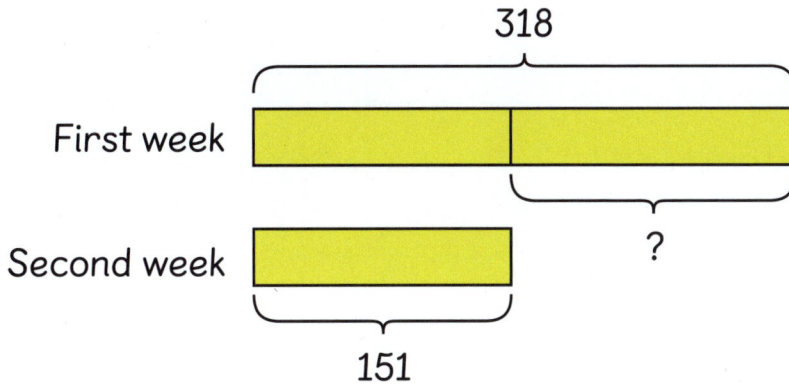

318

First week

Second week

?

151

The snack bar sold ⬚ more burgers in the first week than in the second week.

(b) There is a diner on the same street as the snack bar.
The diner sold 272 burgers in the first week.
How many more burgers did the snack bar sell than the diner in the first week?

The snack bar sold ⬚ more burgers than the diner in the first week.

Subtracting with Renaming (Part 3)

Starter

In the late evening, 830 black crows settle down in the woods to roost for the night. In the early morning, 367 crows fly away.

When crows or other birds settle for the night we call it roosting.

How many crows are still roosting in the woods?

Example

We need to subtract 367 from 830.

There are not enough ones or tens to subtract from.

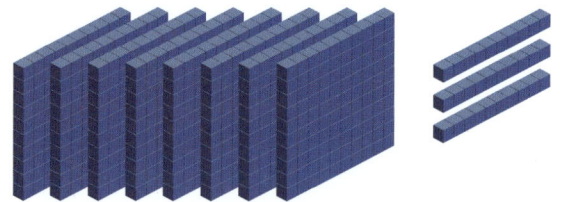

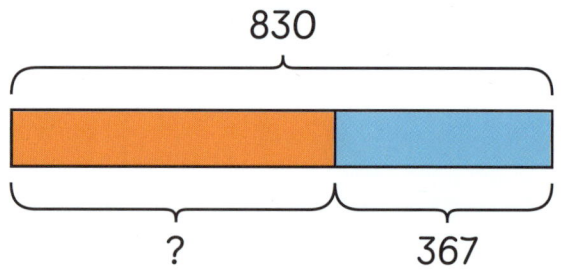

830

? | 367

38

We can take 1 hundred from the 8 hundreds and rename it. We will then have enough ones and tens to subtract 367.

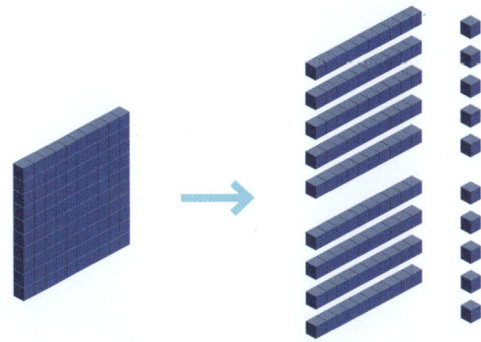

Subtract 367 from 830.

Step 1   Rename 1 ten into 10 ones.

10 ones − 7 ones = 3 ones

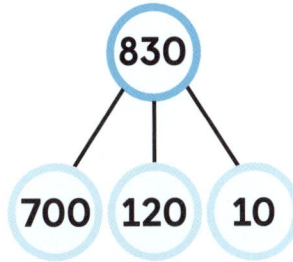

830

700   120   10

```
    h    t    o
            2    10
    8    3̸    0̸
−   3    6    7
_____
              3
```

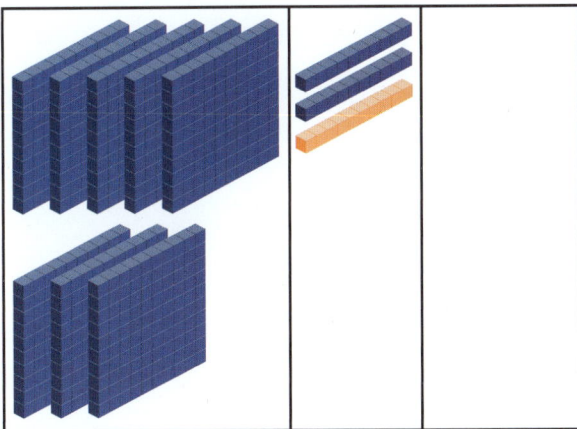 →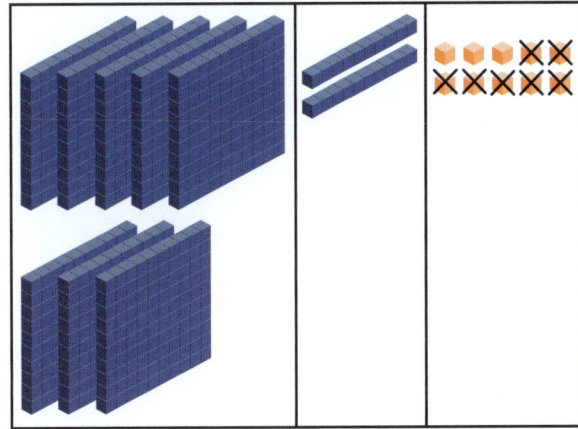

Step 2   Rename 1 hundred into 10 tens.
Subtract the tens.

12 tens − 6 tens = 6 tens

```
    h      t     o
    7     12 7   10
    8̸     3̸    0̸
−   3      6     7
_____
           6     3
```

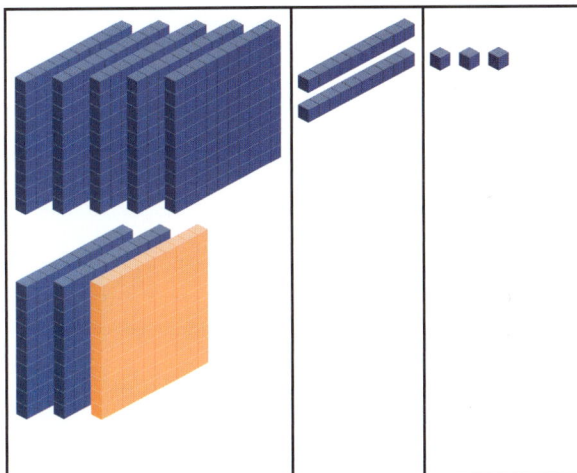 →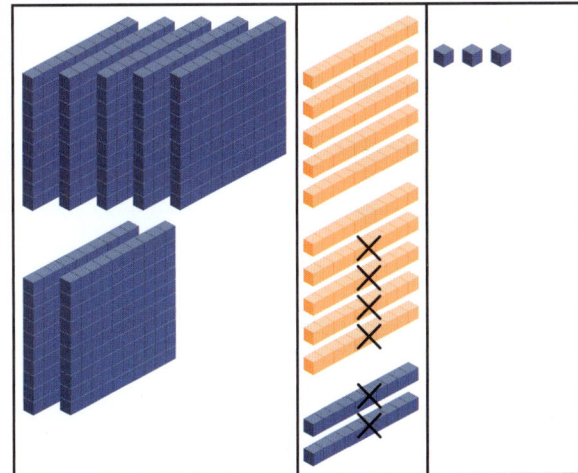

39

Step 3 Subtract the hundreds.

7 hundreds − 3 hundreds = 4 hundreds

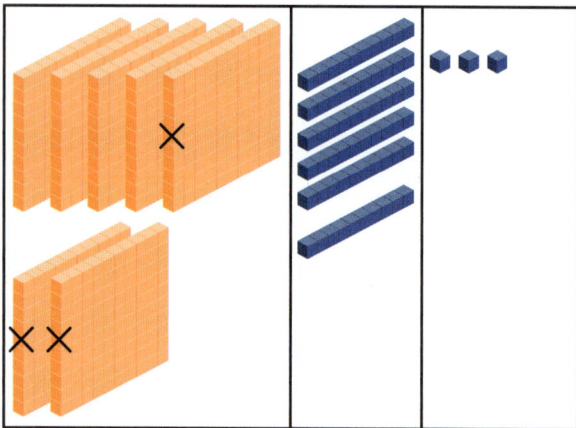

$$
\begin{array}{r}
{}^{7}\!\!\not{8} \quad {}^{12}\!\!\not{3}\!\!\not{3} \quad {}^{10}\!\!\not{0} \\
-\ 3\quad 6\quad 7 \\
\hline
4\quad 6\quad 3
\end{array}
$$

830 − 367 = 463

There are 463 crows still roosting in the woods.

Practice

1 Subtract.

(a)

h	t	o
7	2	6
−	3	8
☐	☐	☐

(b)

h	t	o
8	5	2
−	7	7
☐	☐	☐

(c)

h	t	o
6	3	3
− 3	8	5
☐	☐	☐

(d)

h	t	o
2	2	4
− 1	5	6
☐	☐	☐

(e)

h	t	o
3	0	3
− 2	0	4

(f)

h	t	o
7	0	5
− 6	2	6

(g)

h	t	o
9	0	0
− 5	4	9

(h)

h	t	o
6	0	0
− 4	7	1

2 Emma scored 206 points in her video game on Tuesday.
On Wednesday, she scored 28 points less than she scored on Tuesday.
How many points did Emma score on Wednesday?

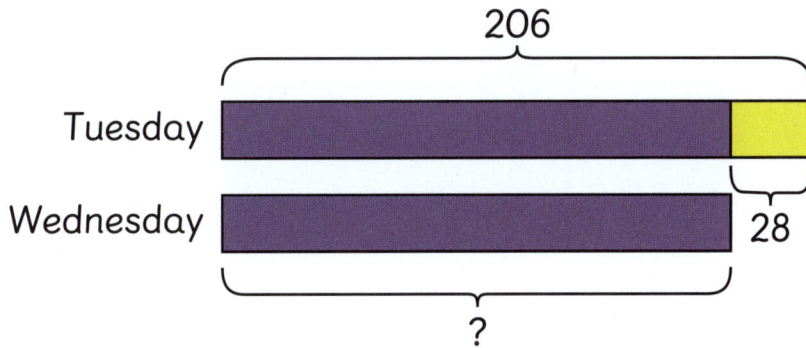

206

Tuesday

Wednesday   28

?

Emma scored ____ points on Wednesday.

Review and Challenge

1   Count in hundreds, tens, and ones.

Fill in the blanks.

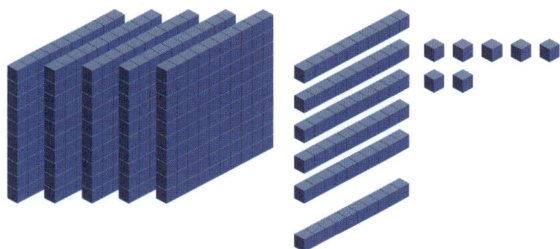

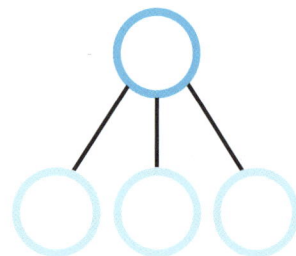

h	t	o

[ ] = [ ] hundreds + [ ] tens + [ ] ones

[ ] = [ ] + [ ] + [ ]

The value of the digit 5 is [ ] .

The digit 7 stands for [   ] .

The digit [ ] is in the tens place.

2   (a)   Write the words in numerals.

eight hundred and sixty-four [ ]

(b)   Write the number in words.

723 [ ]

3 Put the numbers in order from greatest to least.

(a) 579, 521, 920

[ ] , [ ] , [ ]

(b) 559, 641, 425

[ ] , [ ] , [ ]

4 Put the numbers in order from least to greatest.

(a) 373, 725, 223

[ ] , [ ] , [ ]

(b) 747, 338, 350

[ ] , [ ] , [ ]

5 Add or subtract using mental math strategies.

(a) $6 + 9 =$ [ ]

(b) $12 + 5 =$ [ ]

(c) $8 + 8 =$ [ ]

(d) $3 + 14 =$ [ ]

(e) $15 - 4 =$ [ ]

(f) $14 - 6 =$ [ ]

(g) $18 - 5 =$ [ ]

(h) $12 - 5 =$ [ ]

6 Add.

(a) $23 + 51 + 69 =$ [ ]

(b) $85 + 79 + 48 =$ [ ]

(c) $13 + 31 + 29 + 57 =$ [ ]

(d) $54 + 80 + 22 + 66 =$ [ ]

7 Add.

(a)

h	t	o
6	5	3
+ 1	2	8

(b)

h	t	o
2	9	0
+ 6	2	7

(c)

h	t	o
2	6	7
+ 6	3	6

(d)

h	t	o
4	5	5
+ 2	5	7

8 Subtract.

(a)

h	t	o
9	3	1
− 7	2	3

(b)

h	t	o
2	2	9
− 1	6	7

(c)

h	t	o
8	5	0
− 5	7	2

(d)

h	t	o
7	0	0
− 3	8	2

9 Solve and fill in the blanks.

Emma and Jacob both sold raffle tickets at the school fair.
Emma sold 563 raffle tickets and Jacob sold 376 raffle tickets.

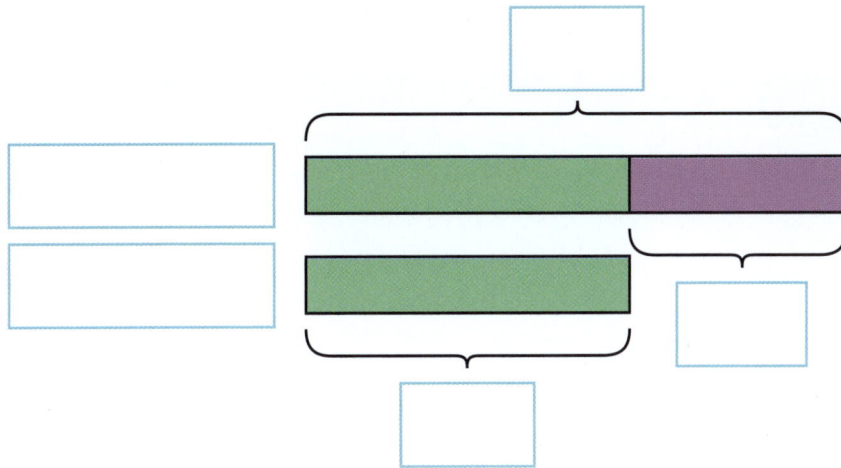

Who sold more raffle tickets? How many more?

[ ] sold [ ] more raffle tickets than [ ].

How many raffle tickets did they sell altogether?

They sold [ ] raffle tickets altogether.

Answers

Page 7

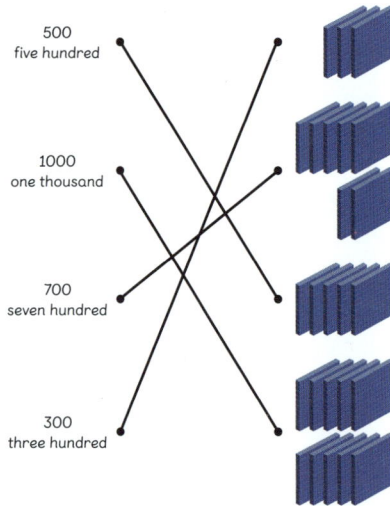

500
five hundred

1000
one thousand

700
seven hundred

300
three hundred

Page 9

1

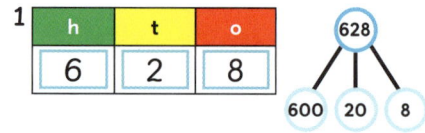

h	t	o
6	2	8

628

600 20 8

628 = 6 hundreds + 2 tens + 8 ones; 628 = 600 + 20 + 8. The value of the digit 6 is 600. The digit 8 stands for 8 ones. The digit 2 is in the tens place. **2 (a)** 768 **(b)** 291 **3 (a)** five hundred and ninety-three **(b)** three hundred and fifty-nine

Page 11 **1 (a)** 765, 756, 675 **(b)** 870, 869, 868 **2 (a)** 389, 391, 412 **(b)** 789, 879, 897 **3** greatest: 976; smallest: 236

Page 13 **1 (a)** 13 **(b)** 14 **(c)** 16 **(d)** 19 **2 (a)** 16 **(b)** 13 **(c)** 7 **(d)** 6

Page 15 **1 (a)** 752 752 + 6 = 758 **(b)** 843 843 + 40 = 883 **(c)** 634 634 + 200 = 834

750 2   803 40   34 600

2 (a) 34 + 5 = 39 **(b)** 57 + 40 = 97 **(c)** 221 + 30 = 251 **(d)** 453 + 500 = 953

Page 17

1

h	t	o
4	^{1}2	6
+ 3	4	9
7	7	5

2

h	t	o
2	^{1}0	8
+ 4	6	3
6	7	1

3

h	t	o
5	^{1}6	9
+ 3	1	9
8	8	8

Page 20

1 (a)

h	t	o
^{1}	8	0
+ 7	2	0
8	0	0

(b)

h	t	o
^{1}2	6	5
+	7	3
3	3	8

(c)

h	t	o
^{1}4	9	6
+	2	2
5	1	8

(d)

h	t	o
^{1}5	5	2
+	8	6
6	3	8

2 (a) 470 + 50 = 520 **(b)** 150 + 56 = 206 **(c)** 281 + 41 = 322 **(d)** 74 + 635 = 709 **(e)** 67 + 272 = 339 **(f)** 325 + 92 = 417 **(g)** 552 + 94 = 646 **(h)** 795 + 93 = 888

Page 21 **3** 309 children are now sitting down. **4** Elliott has 214 beads.

Page 24

1 (a)

h	t	o
^{1}2	^{1}6	5
+ 3	7	8
6	4	3

(b)

h	t	o
^{1}4	^{1}7	2
+ 2	9	9
7	7	1

(c)

h	t	o
^{1}2	^{1}7	8
+ 2	2	2
5	0	0

(d)

h	t	o
^{1}3	^{1}3	6
+ 5	6	8
9	0	4

Page 25

(e)

h	t	o
^{1}6	^{1}9	7
+ 1	8	7
8	8	4

(f)

h	t	o
^{1}2	^{1}8	9
+ 4	5	8
7	4	7

2 The farmer has 603 pumpkins altogether. **3** The two players scored 364 points altogether.

Page 27   **1** 43 + 20 = 63, 63 + 29 = 92, 43 + 20 + 29 = 92   **2 (a)** 36 + 52 + 13 = 101   **(b)** 76 + 72 + 35 = 183
(c) 16 + 37 + 24 + 51 = 128   **(d)** 82 + 47 + 25 + 69 = 223

Page 29   **1 (a)** (576)   576 − 5 = 571   **(b)** (284)   284 − 30 = 254   **(c)** (419)   419 − 200 = 219
570 6   204 80   19 400

2 (a) 57 − 6 = 51   **(b)** 73 − 30 = 43   **(c)** 483 − 50 = 433   **(d)** 949 − 700 = 249

Page 32   **1 (a)**

h	t	o
2	⁶7	¹⁶6
−	5	9
2	1	7

(b)

h	t	o
7	⁸9	¹³3
−	2	7
7	6	6

(c)

h	t	o
5	²3	¹⁶6
−	1	2	8
4	0	8

(d)

h	t	o
9	⁴5	¹⁴4
−	4	3	6
5	1	8

(e)

h	t	o
8	⁶7	¹⁶6
−	3	0	9
5	6	7

(f)

h	t	o
6	⁸9	¹⁵5
−	3	5	6
3	3	9

2 (a) Ravi's high score in the video game is 852.

Page 33   **(b)** The difference between Charles's high score and Holly's high score is 315.   **(c)** Ravi has more points.
(d) He has 187 more points.

Page 36   **1 (a)**

h	t	o
¹2	¹⁵5	8
−	6	3
1	9	5

(b)

h	t	o
⁶7	¹¹1	9
−	4	5
6	7	4

(c)

h	t	o
⁷8	¹⁴4	5
−	7	5	3
	9	2

(d)

h	t	o
⁸9	¹¹1	5
−	1	6	2
7	5	3

(e)

h	t	o
³4	¹⁴4	4
−	1	7	3
2	7	1

(f)

h	t	o
⁴5	¹⁶6	8
−	2	8	4
2	8	4

2 There are 234 empty parking spots in the parking lot.

Page 37   **3 (a)** The snack bar sold 167 more burgers in the first week than in the second week.   **(b)** The snack bar sold 46 more burgers than the diner in the first week.

Page 40   **1 (a)**

h	t	o
⁶7	¹¹2	¹⁶6
−	3	8
6	8	8

(b)

h	t	o
⁷8	¹⁴5	¹²2
−	7	7
7	7	5

(c)

h	t	o
⁵6	¹²3	¹³3
−	3	4	5
2	4	8

(d)

h	t	o
¹2	¹¹2	¹⁴4
−	1	5	6
	6	8

Page 41   **(e)**

h	t	o
²3	⁹¹0	¹³3
−	2	0	4
	9	9

(f)

h	t	o
⁶7	⁹¹0	¹⁵5
−	6	2	6
	7	9

(g)

h	t	o
⁸9	⁹¹0	¹⁰0
−	5	4	9
3	5	1

(h)

h	t	o
⁵6	⁹¹0	¹⁰0
−	4	7	1
1	2	9

2 Emma scored 178 points on Wednesday.

Page 42   **1**

h	t	o
5	6	7

(567)
500 60 7

567 = 5 hundreds + 6 tens + 7 ones; 567 = 500 + 60 + 7. The value of the digit 5 is 500. The digit 7 stands for 7 ones. The digit 6 is in the tens place.

2 (a) 864   **(b)** seven hundred and twenty-three

Answers continued

Page 43   **3 (a)** 920, 579, 521 **(b)** 641, 559, 425 **4 (a)** 223, 373, 725 **(b)** 338, 350, 747 **5 (a)** 6 + 9 = 15 **(b)** 12 + 5 = 17
(c) 8 + 8 = 16 **(d)** 3 + 14 = 17 **(e)** 15 − 4 = 11 **(f)** 14 − 6 = 8 **(g)** 18 − 5 = 13 **(h)** 12 − 5 = 7 **6 (a)** 23 + 51 + 69 = 143
(b) 85 + 79 + 48 = 212 **(c)** 13 + 31 + 29 + 57 = 130 **(d)** 54 + 80 + 22 + 66 = 222

Page 44   **7 (a)**

h	t	o
6	^{1}5	3
+ 1	2	8
7	**8**	**1**

(b)

h	t	o
^{1}2	9	0
+ 6	2	7
9	**1**	**7**

(c)

h	t	o
^{1}2	^{1}6	7
+ 6	3	6
9	**0**	**3**

(d)

h	t	o
^{1}4	^{1}5	5
+ 2	5	7
7	**1**	**2**

8 (a)

h	t	o
9	^{2}3	^{11}1
− 7	2	3
2	**0**	**8**

(b)

h	t	o
2	^{12}2	9
− 1	6	7
	6	**2**

(c)

h	t	o
^{7}8	^{14}5	^{10}0
− 5	7	2
2	**7**	**8**

(d)

h	t	o
^{6}7	$^9{}^{10}$0	^{10}0
− 3	8	2
3	**1**	**8**

Page 45   **9**

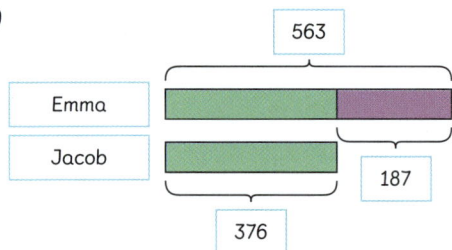

Emma sold 187 more raffle tickets than Jacob. They sold 939 raffle tickets altogether.